T0365454

BEING WITH ASPERGER'S

"SO THAT'S HOW IT'S DONE!"

Lynette Papp

Interior Art Credit: Walter Moore

Balboa Press books may be ordered through booksellers or by contacting:

Balboa Press
A Division of Hay House
1663 Liberty Drive
Bloomington, IN 47403
www.balboapress.com
1 (877) 407-4847

ISBN: 978-1-5043-1452-7 (sc)
ISBN: 978-1-5043-1451-0 (e)

Print information available on the last page.

Balboa Press rev. date: 08/20/2018

AUTHOR'S NOTE

"We are all broken. That's how the light gets in." Whether it was Ernest Hemingway, Leonard Cohen a combination of the two who made this idea famous, Walter's life is testament to it. This memoir takes the form of a posthumous conversation with my long-term partner Walter who struggled throughout his life with what he discovered may have been Asperger's syndrome (AS). After his death I found *Walter's Secret Diary* concealed in a box in our roof. I use conversation "bytes" and photos of the poems, doodles, cartoons and letters within to recollect our life together. In some ways I guess I am using the word "bytes" because this conversation is my attempt to communicate my thoughts and feelings to Walter across time and space.

It was a relationship that spanned over three decades. The little pieces of art, puns and scribbles reveal Walter's confusion and struggle to maintain balance with a personality type that neither of us understood for many years. I have also attempted to express how my life was being in a relationship with this extremely unusually sensitive and creative man. That is why I decided to title it, "***Being with Asperger's.***"

After Walter discovered in middle age that he ticked many of the boxes for a condition called Asperger's syndrome he adopted a favourite saying, "So that's how it's done." He began observing how sociable people handled the world. For most of his life living inside his head was difficult and at times he became mute. He was viewed as odd and eccentric by conventional people but admired and adored by others who appreciated his intelligence and quirky nature. However, Walter did not fit inside the square and found life difficult.

I believe now that in his early life Walter unconsciously constructed his identity through observing literary and artistic role models. He did not fit the "normal" world and needed to carve out a niche for himself to emotionally survive. Generally, he did not like social conventions and stubbornly refused to conform in social settings that did not suit him. Therefore, despite being a talented young architect with a promising career he chose to abandon it and spend much of his life teaching the guitar. Walter's personality also led to a complex personal life with two families prior to joining mine. I have focussed on my own story of life with him and allude to his previous partners as first wife and second wife.

Anecdotes are both comical and sad as in the early days Walter made himself "invisible." Unlike his cartoons, his writing was very personal and seldom shared. It is only now, after his death, that I read much of it for the first time. Like developing a photograph in a dark room, I had a glimpse of what it was like living inside his head! But what a creative space it was. So much wit and talent, and very little of it exposed to the world. Knowing Walter so well I am confident he would be happy for me to share our experience with the many others who live with Asperger's.

Chapter One: Death and Identity

Conversation byte #1

"When I died death died too and I sprang to life anew"

(Moore, W. Musing on death, undated).

After your death I began reflecting on our life together and the journey we took through your battle with Asperger's. My thoughts and these written words are the only way I can converse with you now you are gone. But, let's start at the end.

Gabriel was four years old the day you died. At the dinner table in our nineteenth century villa with a fire burning in the hearth, surrounded by your brightly coloured child – like paintings and eclectic mix of curios family reminisced about you. Gabriel piped up matter – of – factly: "I'm burying poppa!" No one paid any attention, so absorbed in conversation we were. Later, after everyone left I found his drawing. It was worthy of you. Centre of the page stood Bebe (as we called him), mass of dark curls, with a spade in one hand and a bunch of flowers in the other and earth below. Next evening, he proudly placed his picture in your coffin at the wake.

It would amuse you to know that a year later he told me you were not dead. When asked how this was so his reply was: "Poppa is still alive in my head so he's not dead." So, this conversation is for you Walter, to keep you alive in our heads. It is also about your life and mine with Asperger's mind. But, at the very least these conversation bytes help me mourn your loss.

You left a trail of clues – many things I had never seen before - cartoons on paper napkins from restaurants, drawings, letters, musings, paintings, sketch books, boxes of dream diaries, photographs, poetry (of yours and others') and your vast library of books. It was a case of "seek and ye shall find." I felt like archaeologist Howard Carter discovering Tutankhamun's tomb. I made what I could with much of it. Scanning your verses and cartoons, I turned them into photo books for the family. It distracted me from succumbing to the palpable pain of your loss. Yet it was the discovery of your secret diary inside a wooden box in our attic that unleashed a curiosity to follow these threads at a deeper, more extensive level. It revealed previously unexpressed thoughts and emotions. In these I saw a snapshot of the frustration and darkness that at times inhabited your mind.

Conversation byte #2

Making Friends with Death

McCahon still life – like lamps remained on our kauri mantle above the fireplace in the kitchen where you placed them many years ago. They were reminders of your light periods and magic. You transformed all our homes into temples to the various gods – Buddha, Jesus, Vishnu and Shiva and the pagan garden gods of stone and wood. Here you spent your last days amongst your own forest of kauri, ponga, nikau and miscellaneous natives. Always a purist, you uncompromisingly insisted only on indigenous trees. I had to assert my own taste at times sneaking in a potted frangipani or two. It is here we returned you in your wicker basket coffin for your wake.

Your death was as existential and Zen as your life. For you there were no tears, no regrets, no lamenting of things undone. Even though from your sixties onward you had found some peace your response to the doctor's bad news was "I'm okay with dying." From the moment of the reality of impending death you painted the same mountain over and over whilst entertaining an endless trail of daily visitors.

Walter, you had always had a relationship with death. I still recall that dream you had years ago which you named *"Making Friends with Death."* In it, you were sitting chatting amicably with a dark, shadowy, sinister figure of a man on the back of an ancient looking cart. A scene from a medieval morality play, it became etched in my mind. It reminded me of a piece of old stained glass that you had suspended in our bedroom window. Hanging out in your Grandad Jim's morgue seeing dead bodies was a normal part of your childhood, which could explain why. I guess for this reason there were many musings and poems written about death – some witty and some serious. Take this one for example:

"A little death/goes/A long way/ Death is / A Big/ Undertaking/ A Little/ Goes/ A Long/Way."

It disturbed me to realize after reading parts of your diary that your life was so painful during your early days and that you appeared to be contemplating following your younger brother David's pathway out of pain. However, the sad and angry verses were balanced by the humorous or the profoundly wise. Take

1 2 3 and *Death is Final and Complete* for example:

<u>**1 2 3**</u>
We all
Wear
Out
One
Two
Three
We're out.

DEATH
IS
FINAL
AND
COMPLETE
LIFE
IS
UP
IN THE
AIR

These little verses were written in the ***Secret Diary.*** The cover displaying your child-like self – portrait represents you and what is inside. It was a treasure trove of cartoons, doodles and poetry. The cartoon of you depicts your glasses as almost black, and your lips – perplexed. It hints at the darkness and confusion you were experiencing. In contrast, there is a bright sun on the right- hand side and a complex mountain or sea-scape beneath. Expressions of darkness and light are found within. Verses are both humorous and sad, hinting at the deep issues you had faced throughout life. The contrast from tragic to comedic content may have been your way of balancing and handling life.

The secret diary suggests death of innocence and your struggle to grow up. At first I interpreted it as displaying a death wish. There is certainly an element of that in it. However, as I reflect on it as a whole, the more contrasting humorous verses challenge this. The many ideas are so polarized. Consequently, my theory is that the diary expresses your many moods and probably helped to balance you. It represents your personality, feelings and thoughts over many years. Rather battered and scribbled upon, it is another reflection of your complexity – just like your self-portrait cartoon on the cover. More on the secret diary later.

Conversation byte #3

"Hoo Ameye?"

So, Walter, I embarked on a journey of discovery starting on your book trail with the famous Japanese poet Basho's *Narrow Road to the Interior and Other Writings.* Through your collection I discovered your origins from the beat culture. You epitomised the New Zealand Renaissance Man. Kim, a friend, described you as "Walter who wore New Zealand like an overcoat." Through these creative clues, I saw how you constructed an enduring, albeit fragile, social self despite your self – diagnosed Asperger's tendencies and selective muteness.

Born in Timaru New Zealand 1944, from a working - class background, you appear to have created your own identity using great Zen, literary, musical and artistic models. The list is as expansive and eclectic as your music and your rich collection of European, American and Asian literature. There's Basho, the many Taoist writings, the I Ching, Kerouac, Joseph Campbell, Andy Warhol, Derek Jarman, Alan Watts, Samuel Beckett, Jung and Freud not to mention the great architects like Frank Lloyd Wright. To this you added your Aotearoa (New Zealand) identity with friends you admired like James K. Baxter, Colin McCahon, Hone Tuwhare and more. Your classical guitar hero Andre Segovia remained your inspiration to the end.

You spent much of your time reading - reading on the couch after work, reading in bed at night and reading in social situations. You were well – known at the iconic *Hard to Find* Bookstore in Onehunga and over the years collected volumes and volumes of books. Often you had multiple copies of the same title.

Your early appearance was often rather battered – a bit like the diary. Rather unkempt, you enjoyed wearing the same old grey hand-knitted sweater with the odd hole in it and worn brown trousers. Your hair was long and when it was cut it was cut untidily by you. You did not care for appearances. I recall the head of music at one of your schools phoning me as she was worried about you and thought your unkempt appearance fragility. In later years you were known for your "cool" taste, colourful jackets, yarmulke-style skull caps and brightly coloured sneakers. Unmaterialistic materialist, you were truly mutable.

Known for your "off – the – wall" remarks and bizarre ideas, your clever remarks could be interpreted as sarcastic or rude by people who did not know you. When they changed the subject or walked away to speak to someone else you would shut down, feel invisible and then become mute, angry and resentful. This vicious cycle recurred through most of your life.

Your scribbles like "I'm mute Able" are so apt. Anyone who did not know you would think you simply could not spell. Your misspellings, word size, shapes, format and material used to draw on were deliberate. For example, that very simple scrap of paper gives me several messages and truths about your personality. You could be mute at times when you simply could not speak (or chose not to). You were also very able (capable and multi – talented). A clever pun, "mute able" also suggests "mutable" as you had many fluctuating moods and presentations of self. The underlining of "able" is obvious. Recently, I found another piece of self-reflection written late in your life where you said: *I become disheartened periodically and my self-concept fluctuates. I go between thinking I'm great and thinking I'm an idiot. Tunnel vision when I'm teaching can put my student's off. Get over-tired followed by depression. I make inappropriate remarks at times socially, that I think are humorous, but others find obtuse. I make fun of myself and put myself down in front of others. Minimize and marginalize myself - make myself invisible.* (Moore, W. circa 2010).

Existential angst was ongoing as you inhabited your own inner world, but you became less troubled in the years following your self-diagnosis of Asperger's. Angst led to experimention with many art forms whereby you eventually deconstructed art down to a simple child - like form. In reality, a very capable illustrator and cartoonist, you eventually expressed yourself through what could be seen as scribbles and words on canvas. The great New Zealand artist Colin McCahon's landscapes and word art were your greatest influence.

Wherever you lived your favourite McCahon print, worn and slightly faded by the years, mounted on hardboard accompanied you. "The Blessed Virgin Compared to a jug of pure water and the infant Jesus to a lamp." Gluing your name over the word "water," you made it your own. So, it became "The Blessed Virgin Compared to a jug of pure Walter and the infant Jesus to a lamp." Truth in the latter. You were pure. You were simple – an unpretentious genius in disguise. This little poem in your secret diary entitled "Rebirth" expresses it so well:

"Little/ In fact / is known /of our /Origins/ I /myself/ am a distant/ relative/ of the potato."

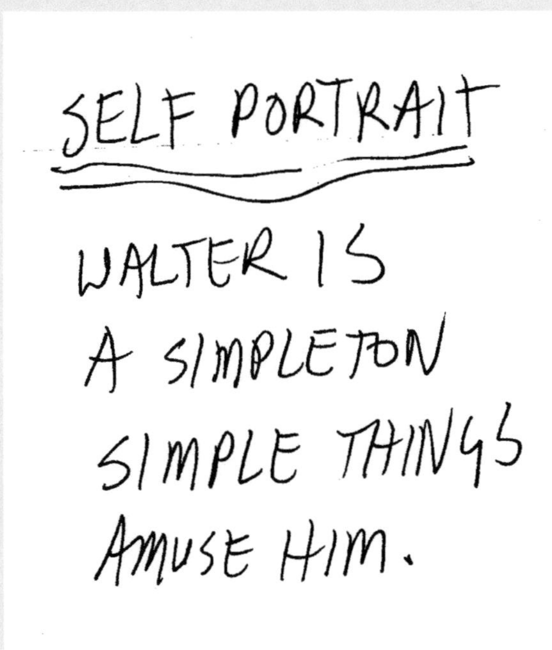

Your *Self Portrait* in words is very telling ... and funny. Those who didn't understand you would have believed it was true. For people you found pretentious or boring you presented Walter as an infantile idiot. Imagine my embarrassment, me being so keen to fit in with everyone, when you morphed into him. Remember the time my widowed mum's man friend came to dinner for the first time. For some reason, never having met him before you huddled, foetal position on the sofa with a thumb in your mouth clutching your Mickey Mouse soft toy. You maintained that façade for the whole evening. That is how he saw you from then on and always felt sorry for me! You could never explain why you behaved in that manner. My family came to accept your eccentric behaviour as – "just Walter" and never held it against you.

Chapter Two: Asperger's

Conversation Byte #4. A "punny" man

When I found your humorous word-play on "Asperger's" after you discovered that such a condition existed, so many memories came flooding back. We had been trying to make sense of your adult son's "oddness" and social awkwardness. There had been many troubled years. His mother had sought treatment for him with a psychiatrist from Australia. Recognising the condition immediately, the psychiatrist told her "the engineering school is full of young men like your son." However, this was the early 1990s and the term Asperger's was not mentioned as a diagnosis. It was not until 1994 that AS was added to the DSM-4 (American Psychiatric

Association's diagnostic reference book). The psychiatrist suggested a weekly routine visit with you and prescribed antidepressants for your son. After that a Thursday night dinner ritual at our house continued for years. Despite these interventions, you continued to worry about your son's mental health due to what happened to your brother.

This concern led to discussion with a therapist friend who suggested that your son may have a condition called Asperger's syndrome. She gave you an article which was the catalyst for the start of important change. On reading it, in a flash of self – awareness you burst into tears and said, "That's me!" From then on you self – diagnosed as having inherited AS. The reason for your difficulty living inside your own head suddenly dawned on you. I remember many times you told me you felt invisible. You would enter a shop and wait as customers who arrived long after you were attended to while you stood helplessly waiting to be noticed. Your frustration often immobilised you and you would become mute and broody. You hated small talk. This was very frustrating for me as your moods and lack of social skills affected me and I had to compensate in the social arena, as well as running the household finances, and was left to make decisions. Close friends and family made allowances for you and despite finding you infuriating at times – so did I.

It seemed you ticked most of the boxes for AS. Your eccentric social behaviour, repetition of the same painting over and over, your clever puns, poems, sensitivity to bright light and certain smells and even your tantrums could be explained. You were different, and so was your son.

I recall we read as much as we could and found that Asperger's syndrome is thought to be on the high functioning autism spectrum. It does not limit the IQ and many AS people are very intelligent and gifted. Neither does it invariably inhibit intimacy, as I can attest to in our relationship. Einstein is thought to have had AS but had numerous affairs. We read an online article by Hazel Muir who quoted autism expert and professor of psychopathology Simon Baron – Cohen. He suggested that "passion, falling in love and standing up for justice are all perfectly compatible with Asperger's… what most people with AS find difficult is casual chatting – they can't do small talk," (Muir, H. *Einstein and Newton showed signs of autism.* Daily-News, 30 April 2003. www.newscientist.com). There is also that "odd focus" where AS people pay attention to stimuli irrelevant to others, like you did to trees and stones.

Your intense interests, moving from periods on one subject, hobby or discipline to another, are typical of some people with AS. There was architecture, music, cartoons, painting, planting native trees, collecting Turkish carpets, collecting glass, photography and writing. Such obsessive behaviour, whilst often annoying to others, can have a silver lining. Because of their intense focus many with AS develop advanced skills in fields like music, science, engineering, mathematics or computer programming. You had achieved a

Master's degree in Architecture and the highest qualification on classical guitar, LTCL. High intelligence often accompanies AS and according to Muir's article, Simon Baron – Cohen suggests that not only Einstein but also Isaac Newton showed many signs of Asperger's syndrome. Moreover, both Baron-Cohen and mathematician Ioan James, in assessing the personality characteristics of Einstein and Newton, discovered there are three key symptoms of Asperger's syndrome: obsessive interests, difficulty in social relationships, and problem communicating. You ticked most of the boxes.

Generic AS websites tell us the condition can also result in heightened environmental sensitivity. This is an aspect I know made you feel vulnerable. It may be the reason we always had soft lighting in the home. Although difficult to read at night, the low wattage lamp light contented you and certainly created an ambience to which I became accustomed. Despite the disadvantages of living with your sensitivities, being with you resulted in transference of your extensive knowledge and appreciation of art and beauty.

Distraction by internal stimuli is also often a factor in AS and your thought processes could be extraordinary. Both you and your son tended to obsess over certain topics in your inner worlds. In conversation, due to hating small talk, you could "cut to the chase" and talk about something completely obtuse. This could be very uncomfortable for the listener who found it incomprehensible. You often complained to me that when you spoke to people in social situations their eyes would glaze and they would walk away. For this reason, you could often not be bothered trying. This can be socially isolating and was one of the bigger challenges of living with your AS.

After you became aware that there were many people who had similar challenges to you, you found comfort in knowing that AS often brings with it giftedness. I always thought both you and your son were gifted. Certainly, the three generations I know personally – you, your son and then your grandson, showed signs of extremely high intelligence. The savant lineage may go back even further judging on feedback from an older cousin. She thought your father sounded very similar. Considered a "black sheep" and very badly behaved socially, Reg was reportedly very clever at school. However, World War II interrupted any potential he may have had. After serving time posted in the army in the Pacific he took on a rural mail run and lived a quiet life in Timaru, drinking and gambling, struggling to pay the bills.

There is a spectrum of functioning in Asperger's and you were on the higher functioning end of that scale and had many friends. But for some, the behavioural challenges associated with Asperger's can lead to social isolation, difficulties at school, workplace and personal relationships. Some of those challenges are the tendency to fixate on certain topics, take idioms or humorous statements literally and inability to read non – verbal cues such as body language or to understand what others are feeling. Some AS people may speak in a monotone voice, have unusual mannerisms or choose unusual topics of conversation. Your speech was normal except for your love of playing with words through puns and your topics of conversation. The puns were sometimes so clever as to be obscure to many. You were a very "punny" man. Your intellectual and artistic AS traits combined with your ability to simply listen to others, worked to your advantage in some circles and you were able to find a niche workplace. Eccentricity is a common and acceptable trait in a music teacher.

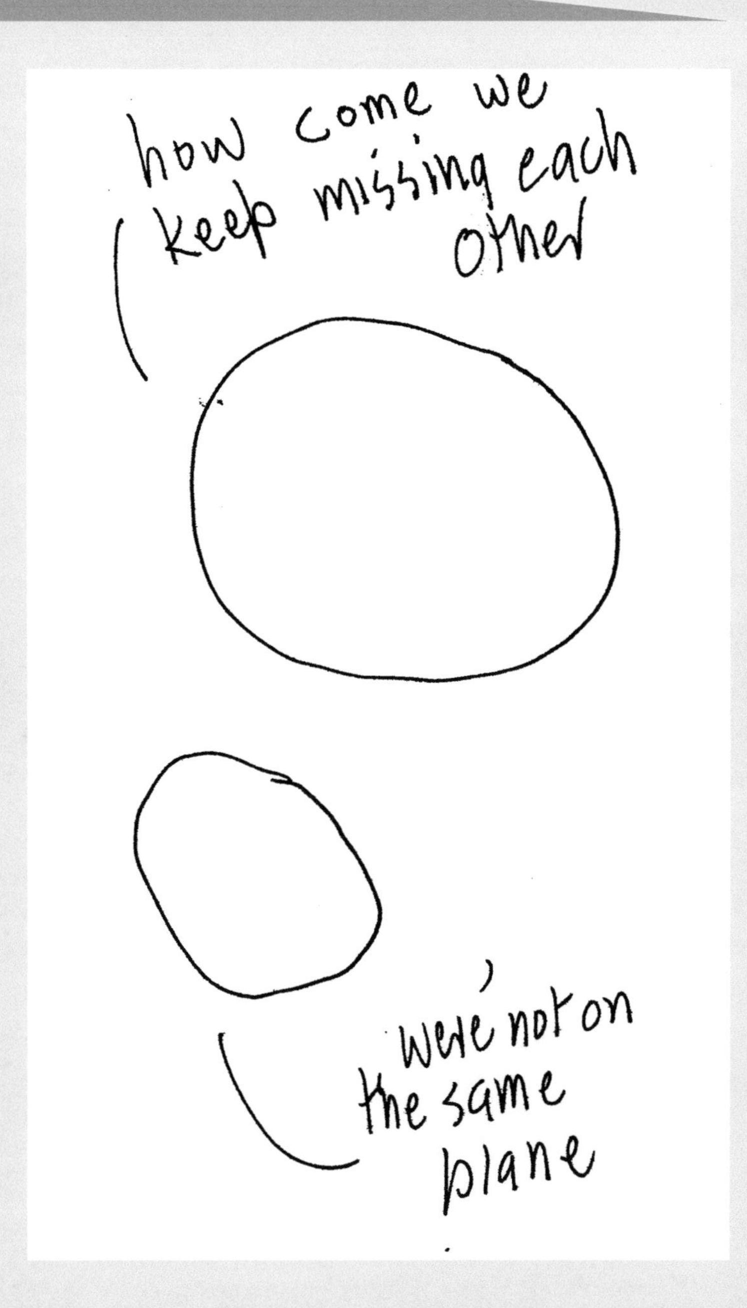

At the time, the information on Asperger's was helpful as an explanation of why you thought, felt and behaved the way you did. On the other hand, it seemed there was little that could be done, no single treatment. Moreover, you had read that social and communication difficulties tend to persist throughout life. However, fast forwarding to the end of your story, many years later through embracing Asperger's as a gift and eliminating alcohol from your life, you found balance.

Having lived with your eldest daughter and her two children, observing how she managed her son with similar traits, I realized the condition can be improved, and the earlier the better. She affectionately and discretely used social skills training with him. Setting clear boundaries, and displaying infinite patience, she encouraged him to use his words when he chose to be isolated and mute. The act of withdrawal, which I often saw you display, is termed by AS therapists as the "acting in stage." The experts in the field like counselling psychologist, Mark Hutten (www.myaspergerschild.com), suggest many ways of working with this such as redirecting attention through cartooning, going for a walk, squeezing a stress ball. You seemed to do this yourself naturally with your doodles and cartoons and your very long walks.

Like you, your grandson had "meltdowns" (tantrums) where he would sabotage social situations. For example, playing board games when it was not conforming to his expectations, he could become broody and then throw all the pieces off the board, ending the game. This is known in the AS literature as the "acting out" phase and is characterised by impulsive externalized behaviours. Hutten's online advice to parents and teachers about dealing with it is to recognise what the signs are and use distraction in the "acting in stage." This is to avoid escalation to acting out. The school placed your grandson in a social skills programme to assist in adapting to the classroom environment. The tantrums lessened over time and ongoing improvement was clear. Eye contact continued to be most problematic. Clearly, specific social skills need to be taught and modelled for those with AS. Having been born post-war, your personality would not have been understood and helpful parenting advice would have only fitted the norm of the time .

I remember a turning point in our relationship that clearly illustrates the need to be specific with an Asperger's partner. We had been together for twenty – five years and you had never told me you loved me. This was difficult, but I always believed that words must be genuine and so accepted that maybe the feeling was not mutual. However, deep down I needed to hear those words. I was training to be a counsellor and staying at the university on a block course far from home. There was an enormous amount of self – reflection and expression of feelings going on for all trainees. One day I decided to send you a text message that said, "If you tell me you love me, I won't take you for granted." Suddenly after all those years you expressed your love for me and continued to do so through our remaining years. "Normal" people tend to take expressing feelings for granted but for you, dealing with the world was very different.

I understood that your brother David (aka DJ's) behaviour was also very eccentric. Your mother, Ada, would not have known how to handle her two unusual gifted boys. Your cousin described you both as living in your own little worlds. Later, as an adult, DJ's behaviour became extremely bizarre after experimenting with drugs. He was diagnosed later as schizophrenic. I recall the story of how he antagonized the men at a party when he chopped a chocolate cake into an untidy mess of crumbs after it had been made with great care by the women. Fortunately for him the women were more forgiving and protected him from any testosterone – fuelled aggression that was about to follow. This could certainly be viewed as "acting out" behaviour on DJ's part displaying what Hutten terms "mind blindness." Mind blindness is the inability for AS people to empathise with others. In my counselling training I discovered that this may be due to a dysfunctional mirror neuron system. Such impairment causes difficulty for people on the autism spectrum to understand and predict social behaviour.

Like your son and grandson, you also had many social situations that were problematic. As well as feeling invisible you often said you felt "stuck." Finally, knowing about Asperger's provided some comfort. There was a label, it could be named and there were many like you and your son. Knowledge used wisely brings understanding. This explained the "thin skin," frustration and tantrums, habitual behaviours, dislike of any change and collection and constant re-arrangement of objects. I recall before you died you burst into tears because I moved a chair from one part of the room to another. You were bed-ridden and had lost control over your environment. I had learnt over the years to allow you full control over our household interiors and garden. For the most part I understood you. It was your Asperger's self, but it was never easy living with your obsessions. I often had to compromise my own aesthetics for you. Unconditional love carried us through the years.

After you died, Sarah who once lived with us, then a rebellious sixteen - year old escaping parenting, recollected ***"I would wake up in the morning, and spotting your new arrangements of feathers, stones and the like, feel like a little child whose toys had been moved by playful fairies overnight."***

With AS came your need for repetition and routine and long binge periods of obsessive, creative behaviour or long periods of inertia. Seemingly futile to the outsider, in the 1980s you produced thousands of photos of objects from the sublime to the ridiculous. Hours were spent in the graveyard photographing stone angels, headstones and flowers. You even photographed dead birds. Very rarely did you photograph people but when you did, they expressed exquisite innocence and candour. I eventually arrived at an understanding of why you kept taking photographs in the cemetery. I'll tell you my theory later!

Your classical guitar determination was also the work of your Asperger's self. No "normal person" could have survived the repetitiveness of what you did. I was still a child during those years when in a rage and frustration you severed your tendons on a knife at a party. You subsequently spent a year painstakingly relearning the guitar left – handed. A gifted pupil of renowned classical guitar teacher Daphne Dobson, it became your passion. You told me you saw a guitar in a shop window and fell in love with it. Eventually you developed your own rest-stroke technique in the tradition of Andre Segovia. Changing hands and position, you purchased a left hand - crafted guitar from David Rubio in England. You attended Master Classes, gained LTCL and set up your own studio at the New Zealand School of Music in Symonds Street where you taught private students. This was how we first met.

Talking to you now about your life and how you came to understand yourself, I wonder if both your grandfather and father may have had some degree of Asperger's syndrome? There certainly seemed to be a pattern developing through your family line – you, your son, and grandson. I recall you told me your grandfather Jim, whom you called Gag, took the family in and you all lived with your grandparents for some time. Intense focus is said to be another AS trait reminding me of the story of how Gag, whilst driving, used to get so absorbed in the scenery that one day he rolled the hearse. Noting that your attention to driving was much the same, I usually offered to drive.

From your cousins' accounts, life was difficult for your mother Ada (an orphan) raising you and David, with Reg for a husband. You told me he used to throw his dinner on the ground if it was not to his liking. His fussiness extended to having his cup of tea made "just so." Otherwise he would not drink it and then throw a tantrum. Reg sounded to me like a spoilt child. His brothers believed he was and the older brother did not speak to him for most of their adult lives. I met your dad only once at the old house in Timaru where he lived with his former housekeeper. It was 1987. I found Reg to be very socially inappropriate and rude. When he picked us up at the bus station he was not happy that you were not alone. "You didn't bring HER with you Charlie!" Not a great start. I recall you used to visit him once a year, alone, and I guess he didn't like a change of routine.

Your cartoon punning the word "more" with "Moore and Moore and Moore" may be unconscious or deliberate. Your family name is Moore. I see three generations in the image because my focus is on a family thread. There are many elements to the cartoon with your bizarre little character having similar dark glasses to your diary self-portrait. However, there is an element of hostility in his appearance. The mouth is scribbled out perhaps indicating muteness, but the repeated words below suggest there is more concealed within. It also has a robotic appearance with the appendage from shoulder to ear positions. Reference to size in your words "smallness is a BIG advantage" contrast the character who is depicted as quite large. The feet give the appearance of motion and rising. Your cartoons can be very obscure to me, despite thinking I knew you so well. However, I believe that "smallness is a big advantage" is a belief you held that kept you from taking any of your talents to the highest level. The idea reminds me of an early word painting you did called "Hiding in the World."

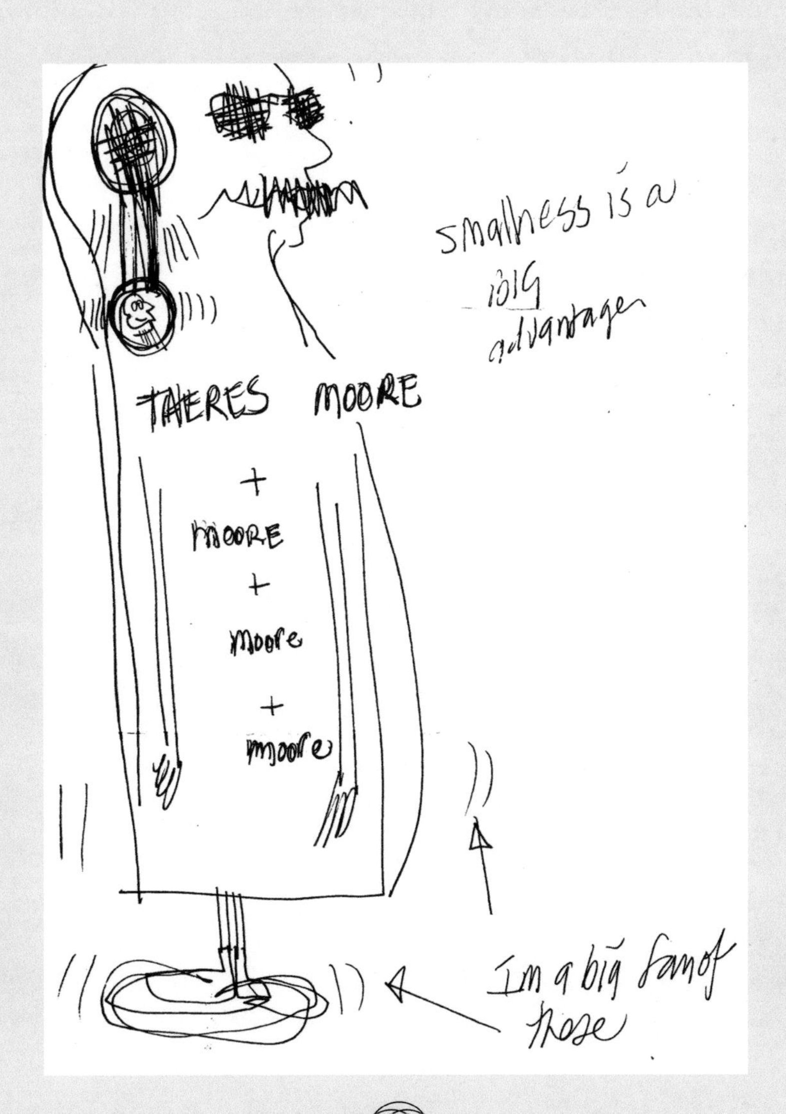

The cartoon may reference a generational pattern of AS. There are characteristics that match. Your father was badly behaved as an adult with few social boundaries. You told me Reg's older brothers believed he was favoured being the youngest and spoilt. Being spoilt implies that he was most likely let off easily and not taught boundaries and social skills. The result was, as a father, Reg modelled immature and infantile behaviour and had specific routines that must not be interrupted. Consequently, to protect her boys from the tantrums your mum would likely have been over – protective and not insistent on boundaries. The social skills training you needed may not have been in place. Older cousin Trish told me that you and David were also very spoilt. Hence, for many years in our home you intermittently displayed similar behaviour traits to your father but in the form of tantrums and withdrawal.

Up until the 1990s children with AS were not understood and poor parenting was often blamed as causing their significant behavioural problems. The difficulty for parents of AS children is the extent of that difficulty. Even the best parents in the world would be challenged raising an AS child. For example, you told me you attacked some other children with a knife when you were a child. You said it was because David had been bullied by them. Being different as a human being can often result in being a target for others. The AS child needs to be taught how to handle bullies appropriately without resorting to violence.

It was only from the 1990s onward that AS was defined and understood as being on the high functioning end of the Autism spectrum. Once diagnosed, some help and support became available. With this new understanding, poor parenting could be ruled out. However, parents of AS children do need support in how to manage. Tantrums and angry outbursts by AS children lead families to feel they are walking on egg shells. Even simple environmental factors such as light and sound can be unbearable for some AS people. I now understand why in the early days of our relationship you had angry outbursts and little tolerance of children. I often felt like I had three children instead of two.

Conversation byte # 5

"I Haff Hexaled Myself"

Doubtless there are multiple interpretations of *I Haff Exhaled Myself*. I see a character in a puff of smoke with a small human or animal on a lead. Again, very obscure, and I would challenge a reader of our conversation to interpret it. It may reference your early years smoking marijuana. However, I choose to focus on the word "exhaled" to be a pun on "excel." You excelled at so much but never took anything to the higher level you were capable of. Maybe that explains the broken line between words and image. There were many years I missed because you were already thirty – six when I met you. There were the Beat years, the classical guitar student days and university days studying architecture, more of which will come later from your first wife's account. During our relationship you were primarily a musician (classical guitarist, itinerant music teacher and multi - instrumentalist). During the 1980s and 90s we had a music teaching partnership. I had taken over some of your Music Centre classes and was later appointed Head of Music at the local high school. Although you were far more qualified than me for that position, I became your boss as your personality made potential for leadership impossible. Our working relationship was symbiotic and suited you. These were very rich days for us. You were composing music and wrote your first musical production. It was called *Quick Fire Nick*.

As an itinerant guitar teacher, you were popular because you taught the students what they wanted. Usually uncompromising with most matters in your life, for survival as a teacher, you moved from purist classical repertoire to teaching Red Hot Chili Peppers and heavy metal. You filled your battered old blue Morris Minor van with amplifiers and equipment to create bands in the various schools you visited daily. Hours were spent writing tablature for your students, transcribing it from tapes. It was much harder then. Now, in our digital world, music is easily downloaded from the internet and schools have their own amplifiers and instruments.

We also had a family band and you taught my boys, Josh and Nik, parts to play on various instruments. I usually played bass. You loved to get live music happening in the house. The riffs were simple, and you persistently drilled us. These were the "good ol' days." There was a decade of that and more school shows. My brother Paul became the drama teacher and our family partnership expanded. Nik also worked back stage on the show.

Before your death, after you were too weak to hold the guitar, you replaced it with the ukulele. Members of our extended family would sit by the winter fire and you would teach everyone the parts. Even my tiny grandsons Nico and Gabriel were given a ukulele to attempt to play along. Gabriel's took the form of a ukulele soft toy.

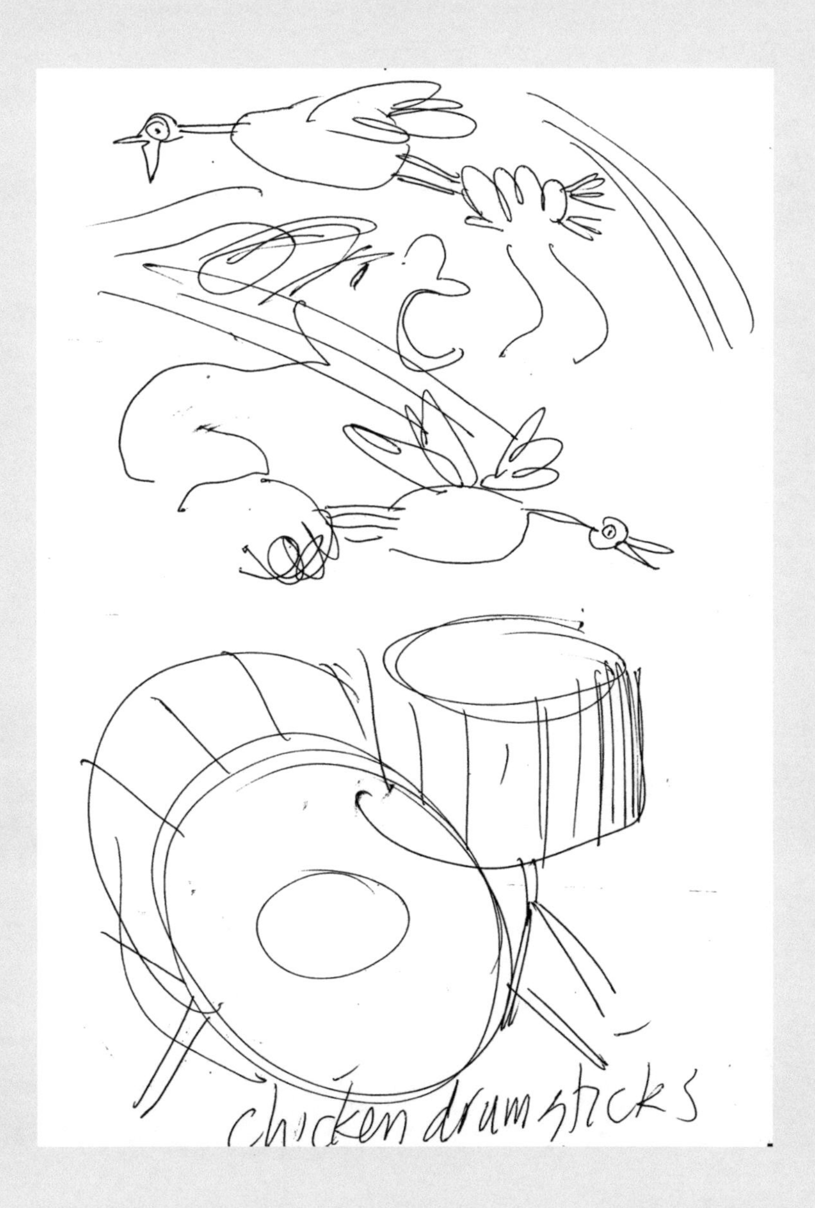

The guitar was your bread and butter. However, it became pedestrian and you fell out of love with it. You became bored. You would cycle off to each of the schools on your daily rounds – a different school each day, sometimes two. You stopped playing classical guitar for long periods and then you would have a binge few weeks of obsessive re – connection.

In spare time you had bouts of being everything else. A creative and talented prolific painter, cartoonist, photographer, dreamer you were a general creator of beauty. However, you would never present yourself publicly or follow any one talent to the point where it could become a new career path. I always thought that design and cartooning were your real talent. Your second wife thought architecture was your special gift.

Your obsession with cartoons and doodles extended through your lifetime. If we went out to dinner you would draw cartoons on paper napkins. Eating out was a compromise and the drawings were your way of spending time outside home. There was no place like home for you.

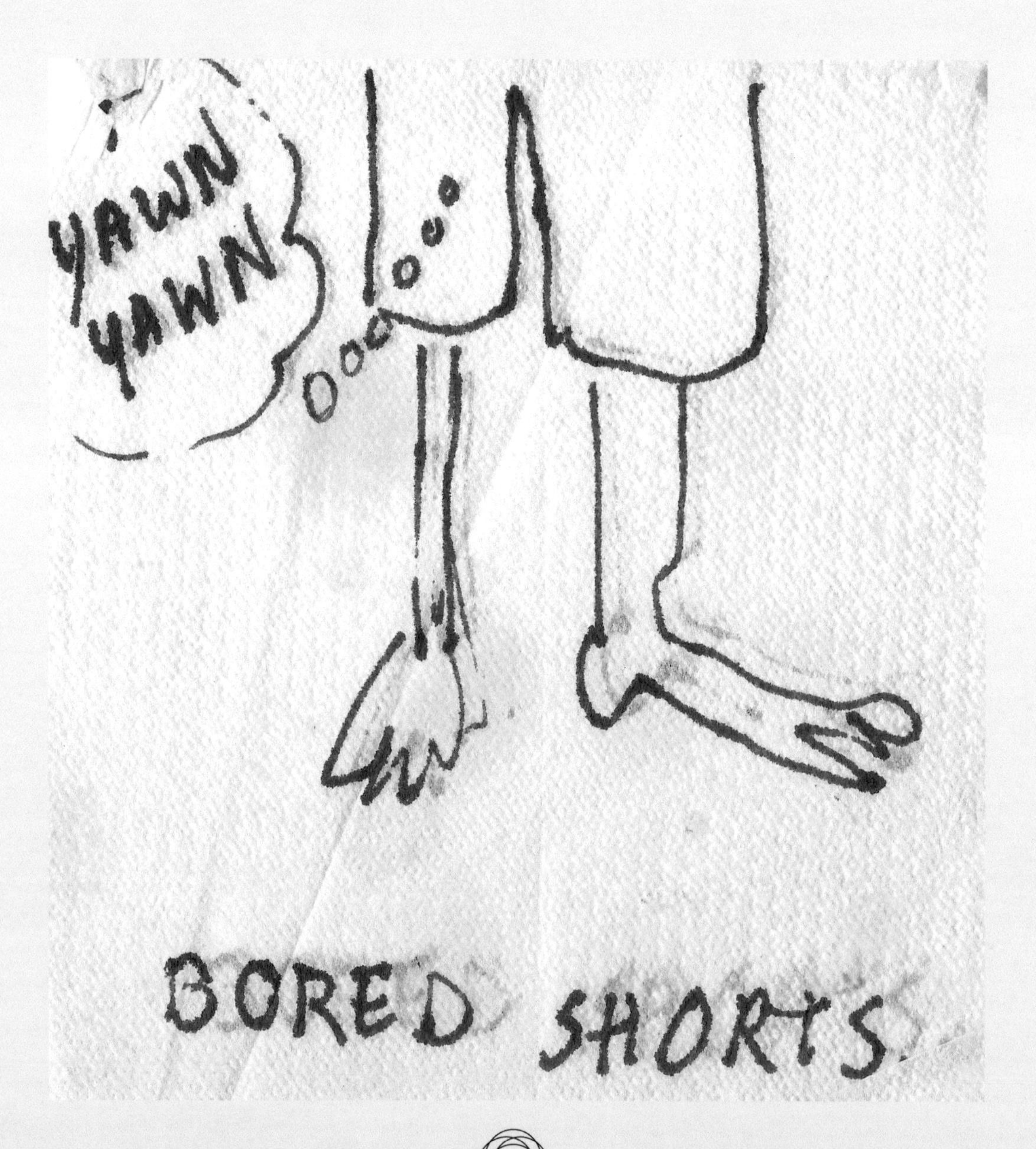

Time in this conversation is not linear and it is impossible to put dates on most of your remaining art and writing. You stubbornly refused to comply with any conventions, such as signing paintings and dating your work. It was beneath you and you did not care. However, I think you secretly wanted to be famous. Your angry reaction to your friend William's criticism of your painting as shallow and meaningless is proof of that. A flourish of vitriolic artistic expression followed in two A3 black charcoal word pictures with large circular scribbles as background:

THERE IS
NOTHING
BEYOND
NOTHING
and
NOTHING IN
ACTION
portrait of William

William, the son of your artist hero Colin McCahon, was your friend through your adult life. In the early days you shared a house and in later years the two of you would walk for hours weekly. He talked about Colin and you listened. You did not speak much but loved to listen. The criticism was the ultimate insult to you and hurt you deeply. As well as the drawings being a heated response to William, they could also reflect your dislike of action. You resented my desire to always be doing something and often criticised me for that. We were certainly opposites.

Conversation byte # 6

"Times of Trouble Burst the Bubble"

The frustrations you faced with Asperger's brought bouts of depression that visited intermittently. You hated small talk and withdrew frequently into yourself in company you found superficial or boring. Consequently, it would be a lie to say we were always happy. Resentment and anger raised their heads many times and I was often left to carry the load.

I recall when you first came to live with me after your second wife asked you to leave. You arrived at my flat with only a yellow transistor radio and your bicycle. Later she gave you a kleensak of your clothes and organised for your two children to visit regularly. You stayed in bed with the covers drawn over your head for days. I felt helpless and did not understand what was happening. I did not know then about the condition that dominated your life. Your routine life with your second family had ended and withdrawal was your way of dealing with change. There was no turning back. That was that. I decided to make the best of it. I am so glad I did. In retrospect I understand, even as a child you could not endure time away from home. Your parents would be called to collect you when you refused to settle into holidays away with cousins. Settling in with me would just take time. You were homesick.

Reading *Walter's Secret Diary,* I caught a glimpse of your inner torment in those moments. Those were the times you shut down, closed the curtains on me and sulked for days on end. You became mute. You self – medicated with alcohol. With alcohol came the anger, tears, frustration and consequently periodic times that I would threaten to leave. In the early years we both saw a counsellor. I often thought about leaving but could never bring myself to do so. Instead I busily pursued my career as a teacher and raised my two boys.

In the company of people who you felt were kindred spirits you could be a lot of fun and animated. However, conventional social settings often threw you and at times your social behaviour was totally bizarre. First encounters especially could unbalance you and you could be very provocative. The first meeting with your eldest daughter's new partner was a case in point. We had just arrived in Hamilton where they were living at the time. He was sitting in the lounge on a chair with his bare feet up on a footstool. Launching yourself forward you bit his big toe. He looked astounded. You made quite an impression! We were all quite speechless. Other times you would just lie down and go to sleep while the dinner or party went on around you.

Times of trouple burst the bubble
+ times of trouble weigh me down
Only slowly is dawning the non-existence
of everything. Still clinging to items
and events as of consequence and
consequently real and not as they
really are which is phantoms whose
import and consequence resides in the
after image – the unimagined reality.
Sunday evening by the fire —

Conversation byte # 7

"I Have No Saviour." Egg shells and wives

The frustration at not being listened to or understood and feeling invisible was intense and your artistic expression and personal journaling were obviously outlets for you to vent. I can still see you brooding in front of the embers of a dying fire in the earlier days at Victoria Street. I would have gone to bed mystified as to what was wrong. It seemed small, seemingly inconsequential moments created a chaos in your mind that "normal" problems or tragedies did not. Our docile old black and tan dog Alex would be sitting there casting a shadow on the tongue and groove kauri walls. You would be writing – silent and sullen.

You were "thin skinned," vulnerable and often living with you felt as if I was walking on egg shells. A little pressure and you would crack. I had sketches, but only two-dimensional pictures, of your previous two relationships. Both women presented me with cautionary tales of what not to do. "Don't walk heavily in the house. Tread softly." "Don't try to organise him." "Don't under any circumstances baby talk." "Keep it simple." "Don't wear lipstick!" I can see now that even these petty criticisms were symptoms of Asperger's. Exceptional women – intelligent and articulate, both loved you and treated you as well as they knew how. They did their best with a personality that none of us fully understood. Both have their own stories which I can never express here.

You managed to express your inner world through art and music, and as you grew older through understanding the AS condition the pain of existence lessened. I had almost forgotten how difficult life was for you until I found the diary. Much of it I did not understand but the sentiment was palpable. It shocked me that you were suffering so much and felt so alone. In your poem, *"I have No Saviour in this World,"* your vulnerability is expressed through metaphor of a new born bird leaving its shell. It was probably written in a time of transition "leaving old patterns" and "taking chances." It expresses the realisation that you are having to make your own way in the world. You were feeling isolated and somewhat broken, "I have no saviour in this world." You were also an agnostic and it may reference your philosophy on life.

In time all things come to pass
leaving the body is not like leaving
the mind leaving old patterns
leaving the shell a new born bird
in a new born world taking
chances the shell is crushed and
broken where is the home now
in the world the home is the world
I have no saviour in this world
I have no saviour in this world
Stone slab shell of a house on the
beach - forced up onto the peopled
land by the sea down stairs

Conversation byte # 8. Architecture:

"the Ageing of a Weariness."

After your death I asked your first wife how you managed to complete your Masters of Architecture thesis on such a dry topic as Structural Plastics. To me you were a creative genius and it seemed incongruous to the Walter I knew. Your "hole" cartoon expresses my surprise very well.

Although I did not know you in the 1970s when I was a student at Auckland University, I had seen what you were capable of as an architect. I used to pass a beautiful office building, painted red like a modern version of a Tang Dynasty building, which I later discovered you had designed as a young architect for JASMAD. It became their office. I decided to message your first wife about that period. From her I learnt how you completed your degree and another very important aspect of your life - loss. I will talk later about the significance of loss. Your first wife agreed that your thesis topic was totally unsuited to your creative nature. It was your tutor's choice. Nevertheless, you completed it and she typed it for you. This was a tribute to the stickability of you both, as she had to learn to type chemical symbols and deal with text that was incomprehensible to her. She also made your graduation gown.

The team effort between you and your first wife is evident. It helped you complete a very dry thesis topic and got you capped. Similarly, we collaborated as a music teaching team for many years. The team effort seemed necessary for you to manage a working life as your struggle with fitting inside the square continued until the last decade. Although living with AS was tough, it made you who you were. The process of the struggle could not be articulated. You could only express it through your art and writing. Nowhere is this more evident than in a little series of architectural concept jottings called *"The Ageing of a Weariness."* You have written a dialogue with yourself showing your inner frustration with the architectural process. The doodled designs show you "blowing your top." This is quite literally how I imagine it would have been. You could not comply with client's wishes. Nevertheless, as a novice architect, you won an award for a kindergarten you designed.

You tended to be uncompromising and unconventional. It had to be your way or no way. In the end you told me you could not stand being cooped up in an office all day. You said you would fall asleep at your desk every afternoon. You needed a niche job, where you were independent. So, when a position as guitar teacher at Auckland Teacher's College came up, you abandoned a very promising career in architecture for that. Your second wife thought this new career move was the biggest mistake of your life and did not approve! I disagree, you chose the path that was to eventually bring you back to your centre.

The "blowing your top" doodle reminds me of the periods when you were asked by friends to design something for them. Because of your stubbornness to conform to what they wanted, you would become intensely frustrated. They would wait expectantly for weeks for your plans only to be disappointed. I wondered if your procrastination was deliberate. Their suggestions would not be followed, and designs could be extremely unconventional. I remember also that our own house suffered some idiosyncrasies, such as the rock staircase you built leading up to the front veranda. It was so uneven that only the brave would use it. Mostly visitors did not wish to risk life and limb and chose the safety of entering through the back door. Nevertheless, the staircase did look very pretty. Aesthetics were always more important to you than practicalities.

In contrast to the confinement of an office as an architect, your new career as an itinerant classical guitar teacher in the 1960s had you commuting all over Auckland. Stormy weather would not deter you and you would ride over the Harbour Bridge from Birkdale on your 1949 rod-model Vespa motor scooter. Your first wife thought it crazy in strong winds. Times did not really change as thirty years on you stubbornly cycled on your bicycle in all weather conditions, including gales, until cancer stopped you in your late sixties.

Being an itinerant teacher suited you as you made your own niche. I recall how the heads of music would give up expecting you to conform. One optimistic soul asked you to write annual reports for your students. After reading an endless stream of "excellent… excellent…excellent" she gave up. You were never asked again. So long as you arrived on time and taught your students in the tiny studios typical of our high school music departments, everyone was happy.

In your sixties, once you had come to terms with your Asperger's self, you were able to express your weaknesses honestly. Amongst your papers I found this self-assessment: *I have a shut-down mechanism when faced with perceived misunderstandings or disinterest by others. I am mildly autistic and have difficulty expressing my needs, and have difficulty making myself understood. I can be critical of others. I also often focus more on the down-side of situations. I don't explore new situations and am a bit agoraphobic.* (Moore, W. circa 2010).

Chapter Three

Conversation byte # 9

The Secret Diary of Walter

I decided that your secret diary should speak for itself. I found it fifteen months after your death. It appeared at a time when I was experiencing the greatest grief. Your death had become more real to me. The diary was a catalyst for that. It seems you were managing your desperation covertly through journaling, the diary and your cartoons. Now, as a counsellor, I can see the value of this for self – soothing or venting in depression and grief. It was also a way around your muteness. At the time, you were unable to express your feelings verbally and this caused immense anger and internalised rage. Your poem entitled, *Song* expresses this well:

SONG
You treat me like I don't exist
And you turn out all the lights
Even though I'm sitting there
In the living room
Reading a magazine.

You make me feel I shouldn't be here
Even though I'm alive
You make me wanna die
But the inconvenience 'twould
cause you would be too mean
You say I look at you like I
hate you but how can I hate
you when I'm not even there.

You say I look at you like I
hate you but how can I hate you
when you know how much I care –

Sometimes I feel like a shadow
on the wall – but even a shadow
has the right to be there even as
a reflection of something more
Substantial

Will I assert myself and be a
bastard or will I** loose **myself
and be a bastard or will I just
swallow my pride, clean up,
pick up the pieces and die.

There is a sense of desperation and anger in the tone of *Song* along with expression of caring for me. You also appeared to be entertaining a death wish. The use of "loose" instead of "lose" is intentional. It refers to both the idea of losing yourself (individuality or death) or letting loose with your repressed anger. Fortunately, those depressive times passed, and, despite the ups and downs, you lived your life in its entirety.

It initially shocked me to read those words – and yes, I know any misspellings were deliberate puns in the writing. Your reality at the time and impression that I did not want you to exist is sad. It was written in our first home in Victoria Street around 1990. After not noticing you were there, I unwittingly turned off the light in the lounge on my way to bed. You were reading and thought it deliberate. In one small action I obliterated you. You took it as a gesture of being a shadow invisible to me, of me not wanting you to exist. A normal person would have simply called out to turn the light back on. But I remember that time clearly, your silence, and recall thinking you looked at me as if you hated me. It was before the Asperger's explanation.

At the time I did not understand the cause of your vulnerability nor what was really going on. Your first wife called it your Black Dog and was very familiar with the story. It was the reason she gave for one day packing up with one year old first - born daughter. She was leaving you and your brother David at the little Birkdale cottage by the sea for the far north forever. Second wife was also very familiar with your moods and depressions. She had attempted to organise you throughout your life together. Having two children kept you together for some years but eventually I think your Black Dog wore you both out.

Processing the verses and ideas, I realized that journal entries are fleeting and momentary. They are part of the thousands of thoughts that flow through our minds in a day. The mood in *Song* by no means reflected our full life together and I was able to let my sadness at reading it go.

Also, in hindsight I know that the look of hatred you sometimes gave me was another AS symptom. It was simply your inability to mirror emotions accurately. You said your guitar teacher Daphne used to ask you why you looked at her with such hatred. We both misinterpreted your inner torment as anger towards us.

There are many other diary entries that are very random and chronologically do not make sense of the years I lived with you. I am uncertain as to the date of it and suspect that you have used a very old notebook to add later musings and poetry. The reason for my uncertainty is that during my period of knowing you, you did not refer to yourself as "Walt." You were always Walter. People who knew you in the 1960s knew you by various nicknames, "Bugs," "Bomb" and "Walt." At least some of the writing like *Song* and a sarcastic little poem to me entitled ("Goo Goo") were written around 1990. The songs, doodles and poetry represent only moments in time but express some of the darkness you were living in then.

The jottings and verses reflected many aspects of your inner life. Although influenced by the ideas of the ancients, particularly from Zen Buddhist and Taoist texts, you were never a follower. Even when we were engaged in a regular yoga routine at the local ashram we attended only one discourse by the guru. Neither of us had an interest in being part of any of the cults that were drawing people during the 1960 – 80s. I think you were a true existentialist and a scholar. Simplicity was the key for you.

What is the secret of life

The enhancing of awareness

What is it for

It's for what happens

You were unwilling to attach importance to any one view. Your philosophy of life was simple – "it's just how it is." Nevertheless, you often found the world frustrating and you could be very intolerant and critical of others.

Simple Sigh Man is a pun on the children's nursery rhyme, *Simple Simon*. It may appear simple but again it is multi-layered and significant. The word "sigh" relates to your frustration, resignation or both. At the time, you saw yourself as a child and never felt quite grown up. Walter, you underrated your own intelligence and often gave the impression of being empty headed. One of your favourite sayings was, "I haven't enough room in my head for this." However, those who knew you well knew how complex and brilliant you really were. I must admit, though, you covered your intellect well when you could not be bothered.

One of your stand – out traits was that you were often intensely moved to tears. Those tears would suffice instead of words. I recall one of the most poignant times in our relationship was a three - day kayak trip down the Whanganui River in 1995. We were with a group of outstanding university professors including the late Dr. Judith Binney, Sebastian Black, Dr. Michael Neil and others. It was organised by close friends and we were guided by Maori elder, Niko Tangaroa who died one year later. We stayed at marae (Maori meeting house) along the way. This was a very political time in New Zealand race relations and Niko took us to Moutoa Gardens which Maori were occupying for seventy-nine days in protest at historic colonial land acquisitions. The professors, all eloquent scholars, spoke with absolute brilliance there, but you simply wept. Your expression of intense emotion was enough to give you mana (respect).

You also brought humour to the trip with your nocturnal snoring. Eventually we were given a little tent of our own so as not to keep everyone awake on the marae. Nik and I slept with you outside without hearing a sound. However, in the morning it was clear that this strategy did not work when Michael popped his head in the tent and said, "Well Walter, you really outdid yourself last night!" I figured that Nik and I were safely entrenched in the "centre of the sound cyclone." You accepted the jests with good spirit. Another time a passing kayaker laughingly gestured to the back of the boat pointing out that I was doing all the paddling in front whilst you were lounging comfortably in the back. I imagine you were deep in thought. I had wondered why it was such a workout.

Seeing you in the photo from 1995 with your head downcast as a sign of respect also reminded me of your pink and green hair days. You had discovered that you could use red or green cochineal (food colouring) on your grey hair. It was not until the principal at one of the high schools asked you to remove the green colouring, that you reverted to normal grey. I guess you valued your job more than your image at that time.

A man of many contrasts, your views could be quite contradictory. Your poem below expressing what you thought about knowledge and understanding is a case in point. You say that "understanding is a sin and ignorance is bliss," but I know predominantly that was not true of you. You were extremely well educated and well – read. I expect that you were expressing your disappointment in the worst aspects of humanity in the moment.

Understanding is a sin
and ignorance is bliss
Understanding is a sin
indeed if all we
understand is this –
God preserve me from
the fools who haunt
me night and day.

I struggled with your secret diary because despite living with you for more than thirty years I could not relate some of the ideas in it to the Walter I knew. Even your handwriting appeared to be from two different people. I know you had to relearn the guitar and write with your opposite hand after surgery, so this probably explains my dilemma. I also realized I have been reading a collection of writing spanning the 1960s until recent time. The page pondering death of innocence refers to your Beat Culture days. The use of the 1960s phrase "digging the world" expressing your youthful freedom is a give-away. It is influenced by Kerouac particularly with the its lack of punctuation and reference to wandering. The poem also triggers my memory of you telling me you often felt like an imposter in your body. You never felt like a real grownup.

I used to read Jack Kerouac
when I was asked and still read
him now though I'm a lot older
and he's a lot older and things
have changed and I'm no longer
a thinking student of Zen and
architecture although I never felt
like one of those just wandering and
lonely digging the world and
all was wonder and mystery and
now it's cold and death looks
in the door – that huge chunk of
knowing which is death, the real
death is death of innocence after that
there ain't no more.

Conversation byte # 10

Black Dog

I think your depressions often created distortions in how you perceived me, and we had some periods of imbalance, spiralling sadness and anger. You responded with what you called your "sins of omission" and I retaliated with "sins of commission." I would take my small boys and leave for a short time. We struggled to keep a grip on each other. It was difficult for you to cope with change at the best of times and my children posed further challenges. Hard enough to be a dad to your own let alone someone else's children. I had to balance your need to be centre stage with the responsibilities of being a mum. You slept a lot. Nik's childhood memory is of you sleeping on the sofa every afternoon. To blot out the hum drum existence of the work a day world and family life, you began to drink. A bottle of wine or two became a daily habit. There was more if friends visited. Your cartoons express your boredom with the mundane and your irritation with family life.

Many of your verses and musings in the secret diary were scribbled out like the sarcastic little piece entitled ***Little Poem for Lynette – Goo goo gaga.*** The title speaks for itself. I guess the moment had passed and you were no longer angry with me.

Your diary brought the memories back. It was good to have a balanced view of you as grief can distort memory and I had put you on a pedestal. Relationships are never black and white and our one was passionate, vivid and technicolour. I sometimes wondered whether you turned to alcohol because I travelled overseas periodically. The longest trip was six weeks backpacking with my brother Paul around South America. On my return I thought you had wasted away. You had become so thin and had not taken care of yourself. I vowed I would never again leave you alone - but I did. Shorter periods. You refused to travel as you had had a portentous dream in your youth that you would die if you went overseas. It kept you landlocked until I finally persuaded you to travel with me to Rarotonga the year before you died.

The trip took place after you had already developed Sino – Malignant Melanoma. The Rarotonga trip was the experience of a lifetime for both of us. For me it was because you were travelling with me at last and for you because it was your one and only. You realized that home was not a place, it was anywhere we were together. The adage, "home is where the heart is" is so true. You were in your last months, but we did not know it at the time. A craniotomy and subsequent radiation treatment soon followed our return home.

Conversation byte # 11 St Francis and your early adult years

After your deat-h all memory of bad times became erased and I elevated you to sainthood. Whilst organising your papers I found a strange little ditty. Many of the poems and jottings were from the 1960s and I did not know their context. Pete, the Anthropologist, was your companion back then. You were friends at university before he left New Zealand to take up a position at the University of Virginia Anthropology Department. He enlightened me on *St. Francis* when he viewed the collection of your writing.

"The Gospel according to Pete" claims that you had a period where you portrayed yourself as St. Francis. No one took you seriously until one day he and mates found you very still with a seagull standing on your head. He also recounted how the two of you frequented coffee bars in the early 1960s doing poetry readings to music. Opposites attract, and you and Pete were certainly that! You, the silent one, would play the saxophone and Pete, the extrovert, would read. He thought it was a great way to attract women. He said you were a bit of a guru then, but the girls soon saw through you.

Although not a ladies' man, I noticed that women were drawn to you because of your sensitivity and innocence. Your silence was interpreted as depth. When I asked about relationships you had as a teen you recounted how you played cowboys and Indians until you were seventeen. Even our relationship began innocently, through friendship. Almost accidentally, it evolved over a one - year period and no words spoken. Chaos was unleashed for a time as two relationships were wrecked. But that was 1980 and St. Francis was the 60s.

I had never heard about that 60s period from you except that you were living out in the sun porch at the School of Architecture until caught and "given the boot." Part - time you worked on building sites where you were called "Bomb." A Beat radical, you loved living outside the square. I so enjoyed hearing those stories. In a conversation I had with your second wife she said she was your girlfriend before you met your first wife. You met when she was living at a student hall of residence and you were camping in the sunporch at the School of Architecture. Returning home for the holidays, on arrival back in Auckland she found you in a new relationship. You simply said, "I'm with Jackie now." Your mother had just died, and you were twenty years old. It must have been about 1964.

In the 1960s you used to work on shearing gangs and complained that you could never get the sheep into the pen. This became a metaphor for your failure later to control classes as a teacher. The pattern continued throughout your life. Always frustrated as an itinerant guitar teacher, you never ever got it under control to your satisfaction. At the end of the day at home you would literally "blow your top." You also kept reflections back then which indicates you used verse and jottings to maintain balance. The following one dated 1962 was in upper case large letters, in black ink on parchment. It shows that you could gain perspective through writing:

YOU HAVE TO SEE
HOW THINGS FEEL
HOW THINGS LOOK
WHEN
YOU'RE IN A DIFFERENT
MOOD
THEN YOU MIGHT
KNOW IF
YOU'RE COMPLAINING
OR
SAYING SOMETHING
I DON'T KNOW ANYTHING
AND THAT'S
ALL
THE WISDOM
THERE IS

I never did see the living rough side of you. By the time I met you, you enjoyed a stable home with simple but aesthetically beautiful surroundings and had worked very hard to buy your first house, a 1930s bungalow in Jordan Avenue. It was the beginning of your planting of indigenous trees period. There were beautiful little grasses and native shrubs but also many that were to become forest giants. The only hint of St. Francis that I saw was your collection of tiny finches and quail. You constructed elegant free – standing aviaries out of delicate timber and mesh. These graced the living rooms of your homes over the years. I must admit to a menagerie of animals at our first house, the nineteenth century villa on almost half an acre at Victoria Street. Just around the corner from your first house, we had dogs, cats, ducks, chickens and frogs. The excuse was that they were for the boys to play with but when I reflect on that now, this fits nicely with your St. Francis image.

Conversation byte # 12

Rituals

Your rituals were more obvious. Things had to be done in a certain manner and you had habitual behaviour that had to be maintained. Years prior to our meeting there were the Japanese tea ceremonies. In the twenty- first century you again took up tea ceremonies on Thursdays with your Chinese flautist friend Peter. He would bring you top quality green tea on his return from holidays in China and you would discuss philosophy. There were also the ritual dinners. Thursday evening for years, almost without fail, your son came to dinner and you cooked the same dish – corned beef, carrots, cabbage, potatoes and peas. In his thirties after his first relationship began, the ritual continued until you became too ill. From time to time you might be persuaded to change track and for a few weeks you would cook chicken. Always too much, you were magnanimous in everything you did. It was always the same. You once told me "there's no success like excess!"

There were also those garden coffee ceremonies in the little Zen courtyard you created at Jordan Avenue where you lived with your second wife. It was an exquisite little garden composed of rocks and delicate native New Zealand grasses. There would be camembert cheese and biscuits and your special coffees. The coffee making was an art-form- in- itself. Made in a pewter jug, steeped then sieved you would pour cream over the back of a teaspoon making a delicious thick layer on top. The neighbourhood women would come to sit and chat. You would say little. You might listen to the gossip or perhaps do some weeding of your native grasses growing between the rocks while you sat there. Maybe a bit of a guru even then, you provided the place to be. It was just good being with you.

I will never forget the hilarious story you told me about your reaction to second wife getting a job for the first time since having children. She wore lipstick. Rather than using words, as a gesture of disapproval you painted lipstick on your own mouth. Forgetting you had it on, you carried on with your morning, and eventually went outside to sunbathe in your underpants. Soon after, a group of architecture students arrived with their lecturer to look at your garden. You had forgotten they were coming but impassively, wearing only your undies and sporting red lipstick, you took them on a tour of your unique native garden. The image of Frankenfurter from *The Rocky Horror Picture Show* springs to my mind here. It still makes me chuckle!

The wine years followed. Only the best wine was served. It was expensive. Wine was replaced by triple lattes at the local café *Brick by Brick* after you suddenly decided to stop drinking alcohol. It is serendipitous that the cafe was in the exact position of the demolished liquor store at Tin Tacks Corner you had visited daily to buy your wine. How very Asperger's! I joined you in the daily coffee ritual. In later years our yoga friends Ena and Mike became companions in discussing philosophy, mysticism and life in a Saturday coffee ritual.

The Japanese café owner hung one of your paintings on the wall. It was simple, so Zen and appropriate. For weeks after your death he honoured your memory placing your triple latte, free of charge, on my table. Ritual is so very Japanese, and you fitted his tradition well. My first husband, Bruce, affectionately called you "The Zen Master" and played guitar at your funeral.

With your accepting, existential nature you were even able to negotiate the rocky terrain of relationship breakup in a Zen way. Bruce became your brother, not an "ex". You always said he reminded you of brother David somehow. The good relations extended to your first wives also. In the school holidays we would stay in the country with second wife and your two children after she married again. Occasionally, we visited first wife in the far north, but distance made those journeys rare. The children and grandchildren have all benefitted from your inclusive, extended whanau style.

Throughout your life you had other friends who you visited on the same day most weeks. A real routine. I recall your visits to Alan who was caretaker at the inner -city cemetery where you would sit and chat for hours sipping tea and enjoying his native planting. William was your weekly walking friend and then there was John, Roger and Andy. These men were all artists and writers, also unconventional and you had time for them.

Chapter Four: Balancing

Conversation byte # 13

Loss: Only the Lonely

A relationship you talked about in more depth was that with your younger brother, David. His suicide occurred a few months before we met. Your first wife had a theory that each of your relationships with the three women in your life followed closely on the heels of a great loss. You started your relationship with her following the early death of your mother. You felt guilty for the rest of your life for not visiting your mother the Christmas before she died. Your second wife joined you at Island Bay soon after first wife left and then we met four months after David's death.

In retrospect I realize that in the early days the time your Black Dog visited us mostly was in a grief you did not have the spoken words to express. The "hole" cartoons, as witty and clever as they are, belie the grief you held. The hole is both the universal concept of all mankind (whole) and the deep hole of loss. Those hours in the 1980s wandering around graveyards taking photographs of angels now make sense. This habitual behaviour and those strangely beautiful photographs of angels, sarcophagi and headstones were your way of dealing with unresolved grief over David. You could not find his grave again. Many occasions I searched with you. However, I have made some peace with him for you now after your death. I think it will make a good conversation before we end.

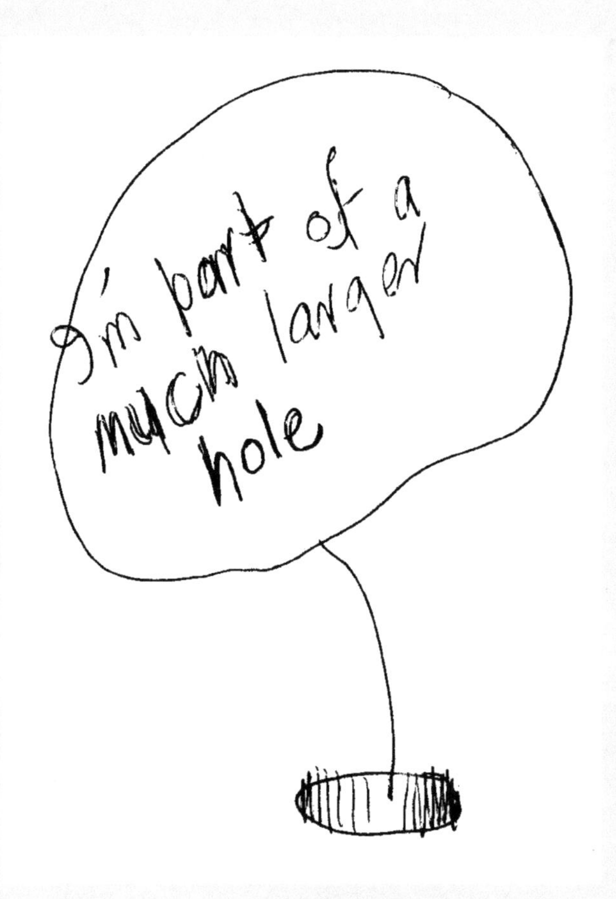

At times David lived with you and you must have experienced his torment at a depth you could not express openly. You told me you felt nothing. His many suicide attempts and bizarre anti - social behaviour left its mark on you, though. When we finally visited the communal land share he left you at Port Fitzroy on Great Barrier Island, thirty years after his suicide, you finally felt it. I shared your grief at this time.

One of David's unsuccessful attempts to kill himself was in that place. He had leapt off a cliff. You stood with my son and I on the rock from which he jumped. It was very high up. The impact of that moment as we looked down over the tea tree - lined slope that he skimmed across became palpable. The doctor who treated him shared an anecdote later. When she asked what he was trying to do, he replied, "Surf the tea tree." Death finally came after he jumped from the fourth floor of the hospital following another unsuccessful attempt. After your death I found an enigmatic verse in the diary which probably alludes to your reaction to the graphic letter received from the police informing you of details of David's death. The typed letter was also in your old wooden box of precious papers, letters and objects in the ceiling along with the following ditty.

He fell
on His face
but it's no
disgrace to fall
on your face
that's all the
world ever
does.

I also found a cartoon (undated) that makes a joke of jumping out a window. Your black humour may have been a way of attempting to lighten the intensity of the loss. However, I do not think you ever recovered from David's death. That story was one of the first things you matter-of-factly told me when I arrived as a new private guitar student at your studio in the late 1970s.

Unable to speak openly about your sadness, the diary also seems to be your way of processing the many losses and changes in your life. You did not cope well with change and it often expresses existential pain and loneliness. Clearly you felt very isolated and struggled to find peace and meaning as in *Only the Lonely*.

ONLY THE LONELY
the meaning of the world is light
the meaning of life is what's next.
the meaning of what's next is what's
been before and what's to be.
only the lonely.

Conversation byte # 14

Making friends and influencing people

Names of famous New Zealanders like James K. Baxter, Colin McCahon and Hone Tuwhare were mentioned in passing when we met. You didn't use their surames, just Jim or Colin or Hone, and most people would not have known how closely associated you were. Not a name – dropper, it was only over time that anecdotes about these friendships came up. Colin was born in Timaru in 1919 and was your friend William's father. You met Colin in the 1960s, visited him at Titirangi with your first wife and his work affected your soul. Your 1980s word- art and some of your landscape paintings were certainly influenced by McCahon.

Amongst your friends who pre-dated our relationship were two famous New Zealand poets. They were also influential in your life. Hone was from Kaikohe and born in 1922 while Jim, as you called him, was born in Dunedin in 1926. All of them were more your father's generation but somehow connections were made. For example, Hone and Jean Tuwhare lived in the Auckland Island Bay community where you lived. You were all great friends and Hone loved listening to your jazz collection. You also taught his son guitar. James K. Baxter (aka Jim) was the great poet and guru of the 1960s who had a commune called Jerusalem in Whanganui. You sometimes drove him there. You said he never stopped talking even before he opened his eyes in the mornings. Friends to you, these men represented icons to me as a young English Literature student in the 1970s. They have all influenced your art and writing as I recently discovered. Amongst your precious papers I found a faded, original, typed first draft of Hone's famous poem *Tangi*. He had written in red biro a note at the side thanking you and your first wife for the loan of your Jazz records. The poem was a gift to you on return of the records. I finally met Hone in the late 1990s when we drove up to Pakiri to see your mutual friend, Shirley Gruar (actress/artist), who was dying of cancer but still painting. You took your guitar and we spent the weekend with her and other friends. I found a short poem or a musing you later wrote on Hone.

The photograph of you with Hone and Mike was taken at the Pakiri house you designed. Coincidentally, it is on the land that you and your second wife moved your Island Bay cottage to before you got "cold feet." Change is never easy living with Asperger's! More about that later.

On a humorous note the ode to Hone was written when we returned home.

HONE
When the
cat said
to the
horse how
come the
long face
it wasn't
talking
about you
that's
for sure

I had seen James K. Baxter, Jesus – like, long-haired, barefoot and bearded, walking down Symonds Street in 1972. I heard he had died not long after that. That year I was studying his poetry, especially the *Jerusalem Sonnets* and the fleeting glimpse of him was special. Your first wife told me that Jim was a friend when you lived at Island Bay in Auckland. He, along with Hone and others, "helped keep your Black Dog at bay." Your second wife also had tales to tell of your times with Jim. There was the funny story of when the two of you stayed at the Jerusalem commune with him. Jim had a morning habit of "peeing out the back window when he awoke so the nuns wouldn't see him." It must have made quite an impression because you wrote a poem about him and his "whare fenestrations." It must have been written after Baxter's death in the early seventies. Years later, when we lived at Victoria Street, Onehunga in the 1980s you produced those delicate Baxter sketches in charcoal on cork tiles. The ode you wrote to him shows your humour, friendship, and references his death in the lines "you shed / your spirit."

Jim
the mouth
engaged gear
long before
the eyes
opened.
whare fenestration
low enough
to pissout.

you shed
your spirit
as you shared your
Kai

nothing Hemi
about that
Mate.

Our work and personal lives overlapped in so many ways. In the mid- 1990s I decided to do my Masters in English Literature research on the first published Maori woman writer in New Zealand. Her name was Jackie Sturme. She was later to become Jackie Baxter. Your connection with Jim opened the door for a rare interview with Jackie at Paekakariki. She lived near the wild Kapiti Coast beach. I still remember it well with driftwood strewn from one end to the other. We took a trip there and met her, taped the interview and began a correspondence in letter form. It was very exciting for both of us. Jackie approved my final product which was under the supervision of well – known Maori author and lecturer, Witi Ihimaera. While Jim served as a mentor for you, Jackie became one for me and I received a Master in English with first class honours. Your influence and mentoring assisted my academic and career success. I have much to thank you for.

Friendships helped to balance you, as both your former wives pointed out to me. Being a sounding board for others, there were many other very interesting, talented New Zealand contemporaries in your life. They were diverse. As well as artists and poets, there were architects and philosophers. Your good friend Kim, a Canadian self – taught vintner, built up a boutique winery, Eskdale Wines, in Napier. You designed the house where he and his wife Trish raised their family. You also designed the black and white pen and ink label for their signature Eskdale wine bottle. It depicted their rustic winery. They asked you to do some illustrations of the house in the 1990s and the photograph depicts two of the drawings on display in their home. The house has your spirit and feels like home. The wine is superb. I particularly enjoyed Kim's comments about you after you died. One that stands out relates to the simplicity of your art. He joked, *"I don't think Walter ever got over making his first sandcastle."* We kept in touch regularly from the late 1990s and visited from time to time.

Otahuhu artist Roger Staples was also one of your close friends. He had married your first cousin, Trish in the 1970s. After she died in 1992, you remained friends and visited him every week. Roger was part of your ritual life. Friday lunchtime you would cycle from school to sit in his studio. Roger told me that often you would sit for hours, saying nothing. Just being there was enough in the ambience of his garden studio. You always took the exact same cake from the bakery nearby.

One of Roger's proteges as a high school art teacher was a young painter, Zahran Southan. A gifted artist, Zahran later studied in the style of the Italian masters in Florence. You were such an interesting and unique individual you attracted Zahran's attention. You sat for hours for him and he produced some beautiful early work. A portrait of you in oils was gifted to me after you died.

So, although you were very quiet and often just sat and laughed or cried, people were drawn to you. A good host and good listener, you could be very fine company. The friends included many young Brazilians. My Brazilian daughter – in – law Kellen introduced the first of many to us. They thought you were "cool." Our bike rides with them and our many Brazilian barbecues were legendary. They brought the party back into our lives. I recall your first wife saying you were happiest when Hone and the others who lived at Birkdale were around. You did like company and these young Brazilians enlivened us

You were charismatic and special to so many people. As well as your relationship with me, they all contributed to helping you balance. You were aware of this. You once sent me a letter from Timaru in the 1980s saying, *"Lynette, I know now that you help balance me."* I recall hearing that your friend Timothy left your funeral saying with some dismay to his wife," I thought I was Walter's best friend, but so does everyone else here!" There are so many people whose lives you touched. They are countless. Most of them attended your funeral. John Barnett and his wife artist / designer Lesley Kaiser were loyal friends from the first days we lived together and visited us regularly till the day you died. Andy Palace replaced David as a brother to you and your history with Andy spans decades. You exhibited art together – Andy's spectacular *Metal as Anything* space age lamps and your paintings. Throughout your last months of life Andy visited every Wednesday entertaining you and cooking for us. Andy kept up our spirits. He also did his best to keep you alive using alternative cures. How you dared die with Andy about, I do not know!

Chapter Five: Flow and Integration

Conversation byte # 15

Dream Time: "the Integrated Cy – key"

Walter you were an avid dreamer at night as well as a daydreamer. Anecdotes from your childhood suggest you lived in your own little world. One of the many special things we shared was our love of dream analysis. After I trained as a counsellor I became interested in therapeutic dreamwork. You shared my journey, reading my textbooks and practising counselling techniques with me. Like me, you kept a dream diary for many years and most mornings we would wake and discuss our dreams. It became a morning ritual. Your dreams were meaningful and often pre-cognitive. They were explosions of extraordinary vividness and clarity. Often complex narratives, they helped inform you of what was really going on when you were feeling "stuck" and insignificant. They presented you with emotional feedback expressing what you felt. The dream diaries and analysis helped us both cope with living with AS. At the end they also provided spiritual comfort when the cancer took over and you knew you were dying.

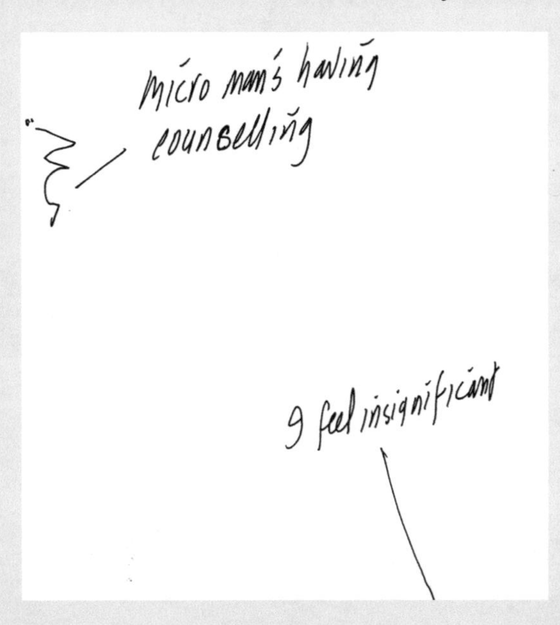

You loved going to our dream groups. Lively Walter dreams energized us all. Since you died I found your dream diaries and there were hundreds of dream-reports over the years. There was one year that stood out - 2010. This was the period in which you met Death as a character. Closer to the year of your death you experienced some exquisitely pure white dreams. The *White Shed* stands out for its radiance where you were met by a bell bird. In retrospect, I think the one you named *Making Friends with Death* foreshadowed your death and cancer had begun. From then on you lost weight and gradually became luminous.

It seemed that externalization of your unconscious through dream content was an important key for you to unlock your feelings. It was enlightening, and I think it helped you grow into the self you wanted. Through it we came to understand each other more and grow as a couple. Finally, in our last decade together we were operating on the "same plane."

As you aged, and I had finally accepted your complex personality, you experienced longer periods of happiness. You were more balanced without compromising creativity. The prolific outpouring of paintings began. We were happier. Old vicious cycles were broken. There were "aha moments." You loved to use a little counsellor's joke I shared when I was training – "spot it you've got it." You read my counselling texts, helped edit my essays and shared my journey. Through our counselling process and mutual dream work you also started to see yourself. You had found a mirror. So, Walter, externalization through dream-work was probably one of the keys to your transformation along with your discovery of Asperger's. You became comfortable with being your AS self. I understood you at last and we understood each other.

Furthermore, in 2010 you surprised me by joining the gym. I had been working out for years and you normally stayed home on the couch reading. As a child you said you used to run the wrong way on the rugby field and so chose not to partake in team sports. For that reason, you generally viewed sport and energetic exercise as pointless, so this transformation was a shock. For months we worked out together and you would jokingly flex your newly acquired biceps. You thrived at the gym doing pump classes. I found your cartoon of us that I think references this huge change.

Exercise has long been shown to be important for mental health. Because AS people are often not good at sport they tend to avoid it, but I am certain it was a contributing factor in increasing your serotonin levels. I wonder what it would have been like if we had that knowledge earlier? How would it have been if your family had raised you and David with the knowledge we now have? Certainly, your art and cartoons helped balance you but what if there had been early social skills training and the counselling and dreamwork had started much earlier? So many questions! In hindsight I now know that knowledge brings understanding and acceptance. The earlier the diagnosis the better. There may not be a cure for AS but knowledge helps to adjust to being different, enjoying the talents that it can bring, and living with it.

A diary entry which was uncharacteristically dated, April 21/ 2012, shows your progression:

the more you
get into your game
the more everything
turns
to
laughter

Conversation byte # 16.

Your "Cy-key" and my psyche

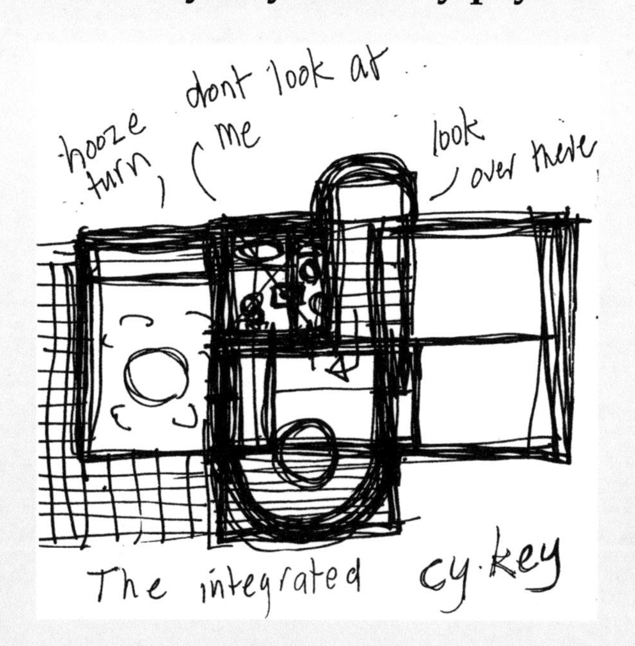

You read and was influenced by Carl Jungs's texts on the psyche. A great believer in the influence of the unconscious process, Jung believed that the psyche is a self-regulating system that seeks to maintain balance between opposing qualities whilst striving for growth. The result of that growth is termed individuation. As a trainee counsellor I was also reading Jung and we began to work together towards individuation. Our dream diaries and morning coffee sessions at the local café helped us process our dreams. It was in the last decade of our life together that your psyche and mine finally clicked into place. Years of struggle turned into flow. It was at that time that you began your *Mountains Flow* series of paintings. These were colourful child – like images of mountains with words. I think these word paintings are my favourites. The colour and life in them signalled a new energy. After your death I read one of your Zen Buddhist books and saw the very words *Mountains walk. Mountains flow* that had inspired the paintings. Over time, the same words were repeated in each painting. Gradually the colours became darker and more sombre as you approached death.

Recently, I re-read some entries in one of your other journals from 2009. In it you wrote: *I'm integrating my waking and sleeping lives by drawing on the unconscious messages from my dreams. And I'm using painting as a tool to draw out the unconscious. I'm a prolific and vivid dreamer. This has considerably enriched my life. I am growing as a person and becoming more integrated* (Moore, W. circa 2009).

You were sixty-five years old, and still a work in progress.

Yes, we had connected in the early days, but your periodic darkness often obscured the light. In our first encounter there was a flash of recognition. A student of the classical guitar, I had heard about you and had fleeting images of you at guitar recitals, but we had never met. When my first teacher moved to Australia he made suggestions of who could replace him. Instruction was that I was to go to his former teacher. At first, I followed his advice but soon found her style did not suit me. I had just given birth to Joshua and was wanting a slower return to the guitar. She was also your teacher and the best around. However, the rigour of discipline required by her was not for me. Instead I nervously knocked on the door of your studio at the School of Music in Symonds Street. That was 1979. We looked at each other and you started laughing. On the first lesson you told me your brother had killed himself. I did not know what to say.

I became the student you said had best adopted your unique technique of rest stroke. You were relentless and almost drove me crazy with the repetition – over and over and over and over! I almost gave up but for our conversations on movies, music and books. I was a primary school teacher with an English literature major at university and had read much of your repertoire. We shared the same interests. We talked about Sam Beckett (as you called him), Woody Allen, Leonard Cohen and the Marx Brothers. In a card game it would be "snap." You giggled a lot. Your eccentricity was obvious, but you drew me like a magnet. A strong friendship developed. We became partners in buying for our neighbourhood vegetable co-op at the markets. A seed had been sewn. A year later we had become inseparable, had an affair and eventually lived together.

Conversation byte # 17

GRANDparents

I woke early this morning wanting to talk to you again about the best years of our life together. What was it that made it so good? My theory, and I think you would agree with me, is that apart from your discovery of AS it began to flourish when you became a grandfather and we became grandparents together. When your first granddaughter was born, life changed. You turned 60 that year. I think some well-modelled grandfatherly instincts kicked in. You stopped drinking not long after. I believe you had a wonderful, loving role model in your grandfather. Not so with fathering. I will need to digress a little here and jump back in time into a little of your family history.

As a child when your family lived with your grandparents, you loved your grandfather, Gag, and spent many hours with him. He was an undertaker, so you frequented the morgue. Unlike me, the sight of a dead body was quite normal for you. In contrast to your father who modelled periodic tantrums, your grandfather became your role model. Gag let you use his tools in his workshop and you learnt many skills from him. He had been a carpenter transferring his skills to funeral director during the Depression of the 1930s. He built the coffins himself. So, Walter, you had a great role model in your grandfather and became a jack – of – all – trades. He was modelling "how it was done" in a practical sense and in being a companion. I was always able to rely on you for practical chores. You were able to fix anything, a real handyman.

As a grandfather you enjoyed doing things with the grandchildren. You became playful. I had not seen that quality in you with your own three children or mine. So, this was a surprise. You played rough and tumble games with the boys and threw them up in the air and they loved you. Digging garden paths and cycling was also on the agenda and we had many happy hours climbing One Tree Hill and Mangere Mountain. I had never seen you so happy and lively.

Conversation byte # 18

Walter and Basho

After you died I began reading your books. They proved to be quite a revelation. When I read Sam Hamill's foreword to the 1998 edition of Basho's ***Narrow Road to the Interior and Other Writing*** it ignited an "aha moment." I could suddenly see your influences in the description of Basho changing the traditional Chinese form of Haiku. In his last years he made his own, honed, pure and simple haiku form using qualities of karumi (meaning lightness) together with sabi (existential Zen loneliness) and shibumi (unpretentious natural beauty). Hamill tells how Basho's life had been profoundly shaped by wabi (deep appreciation of things old, worn, modest and simple). In your art and writing I can see those qualities. In your person, in your spirit I see wabi. You lived in the moment and, although a collector of objects (stones, pottery, glass, curios), you were somehow not attached to the material world in the same way as "normal" people. Because of this unpretentiousness, despite your prolific art work, you were never going to be a famous artist. In many ways though, Walter, I think you created yourself as a work of art.

Your love of simple but beautiful things meant that our home was like a museum or an old curiosity shop. Kids loved coming here. Our grandchildren especially were drawn to it as they were drawn to you. The little cedar shed in the garden that I bought to store junk in was quickly appropriated by you. It became your studio and shrine room with Buddhist and Hindu statues and your teapots and delicate, turquoise porcelain teacups. It was here that you painted your final mountain series in oils. You began playing classical guitar once again and entertained your friends with your green tea, cheese and "bickies" ritual. You found solace in this place. You had come full circle.

Although you had initially resented the move from our old home on Victoria Street you accommodated my wishes and gradually adapted, making the new property your own by planting obsessively. The place became a replica of your other bush cottages and former homes. I remember you telling me the story of how you and your second wife were going to move up north to Pakiri and live with friends. I guess this was somewhere around 1970. You decided to relocate the old, Island Bay cottage there. It was taken apart, placed on a friend's truck and off you went. Hippies to the country. Unsurprisingly, you lasted only a few days before you realized you could not stand being away from the city. You had tried to bring your city cottage to the country – an extreme Asperger's gesture!

Later Onehunga became your place and you - a local, colourful figure. In old age you were legendary as the eccentric old cyclist riding off to your many South Auckland schools toting your guitar and saxophone over your shoulder - long grey hair flying untidily from your helmet. I remember you laughing and recounting how some Polynesian children in Mangere, seeing you cycle by, stopped in their tracks and called out, "Back to the future!" You were not insulted. You laughed a lot. You cried a lot too! You constructed your environments and your intellect in a style that Basho would have approved. Your favourite sayings were "Keep it simple," "I don't have room in my head for all that!" and "Too many words!" I think the following little verse written on a note-to-self page expresses your essence and intellect well. *The Way* is influenced by your reading of Zen texts. It displays your acceptance of your life. The use of the *THINGS TO DO* pad serves as a reminder in tough times. As always, your scribbled over words are deliberate. You are punning the words "loses" and "loose." Although we are all born into the world as free spirits, with time we all become prisoners of our social conditioning.

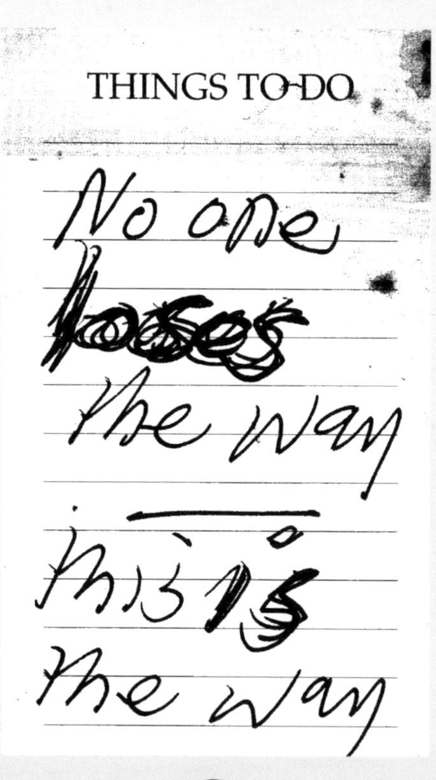
THINGS TO DO

No one
loses
the way
—
this is
the way

Conversation byte # 19

Funeral. You're living in the present

Your funeral drew a huge crowd of friends, old and new. Our colourful, vivacious friend Jude was the celebrant and kept the funeral on a high which I think you would have wanted. Bruce and Jan performed Leonard Cohen's *Hallelujah* and the tears flowed freely. Many humorous stories were told about you, including your first wife's hilarious recounts of 1960s acid days at Island Bay. Andy recounted other later tales. Hundreds of your paintings were available at the end for koha (donation) to Hospice. Most people took one and some grabbed a bundle.

Our principal closed the school for half a day to honour you. When I returned to work having been home nursing you through the last months of cancer, your paintings were everywhere. People had them on their office walls and a carefully selected one entitled *I Love It to Happen* was framed and placed in the staffroom with a plaque in your memory. You had taught guitar at this school for thirty - two years. The Music Department had a kauri tree planted in your honour down by the gym. A little ritual was held for you there and classical guitar piece *Natalia* was played in your honour. By coincidence, *Natalia* by George Moustaki has always been one of my favourites and was the composition I played for you on our first lesson. I walk to that tree when I feel sad. I feel your presence in the kauri.

I wanted a place for your ashes that meant something to you and our grandchildren. What better place than the tree we used to take them to near home. We called it our Hobbit Tree. The children made it their own and have special places inside and around the area where they sprinkled their portions of ashes. Your spirit lives on in all the children through memory. It is interesting how well they adjusted to your death. They saw your body during the wake. This was not a conventional pakeha wake. Usually the body remains at the morgue until the funeral. We were following the ritual of Maori tangi to some degree, making it our own, so we brought your body home. Friends and family spent time with you there and reminisced about you. Seven - year olds Nico and Alex wondered how come you were wearing your "cool clothes." Next morning Nico inquired of his mum, "How did poppa come to be wearing his cool clothes and shoes?" When she told him that Aunty Chris and I had helped the ladies at the funeral parlour wash and dress your body he then countered, "How did nana get poppa to stand up to get dressed when he was already dead?" Practical minds of children lightened the sadness. You and Hone would have laughed and laughed – you would have approved!

It was the best funeral ever in my family. The children all commemorated you in many various ways – drawings, stories and words. This ritual of their own created a special place that they will always remember. There were no morbid feelings. Your spirit has brought a peace and beauty to the death experience.

So now I need to draw a close on this conversation with you, my weird and whacky Asperger's man. After your death I slipped into a deep grief. It was fourteen months after your death when I decided to write this conversation and present your life and some of your work to anyone who might appreciate it, or simply to keep your memory alive. It was then that I realized there was something I needed to do apart from this book. The one remaining piece of your life that needed closure was staring me in the face. It was finding your brother David.

Conversation byte # 20

Finding David and Closure

As I previously mentioned, we had hunted through the cemetery on many occasions in search of David's grave to no avail. Once again, your trail of "archaeological" treasures came to the rescue. I found photographs you had taken at his funeral in 1979. I also found a receipt for purchase of a plot which had coordinates on it. Visiting *Waikaraka Cemetery* armed with photo and receipt, I began walking the rows. Eventually I phoned David's closest friend John who was at the funeral to see if he could help me locate it as the coordinates were difficult to follow. After our conversation I realized that David's grave was unmarked and recalled you had told me he had given strict instructions as to the simplicity of his interment. David wanted to be buried in a cardboard box, but authorities did not allow this. Thus, an unmarked grave made sense for you to in some way respect his wish for simplicity. After that I was able to find the site that had no marker. Placing one of the special stones from your bookshelf and my own tiny scallop shell with the photo from David's funeral, I sprinkled some of your remaining ashes in his honour. And so, Walter, at least a sprinkle of physical you joined your brother on earth.

For me, as I rebuild my life, I have experienced you as light and dreams in my saddest moments. In a dream you came and carried me under your arm at great speed through space. It felt exhilarating, but I cried out, "I'm not ready yet," and awoke. Another time I woke early one morning and perceived you as a light behind your rata vine in the garden by your studio. Ironically the vine had not flowered very much while you were alive but this year it was luxuriant with red flowers. Reminiscent of a landscaper's garden, the light illuminated both the rata vine and your cedar studio. I felt comforted in the thought that maybe you exist but on another plane. But the most profound light was a rare moment at sunrise when your photograph on my dresser caught a beam of light. The room was dark, but I woke to a radiantly illuminated laughing image of you. Although not a great believer in after life, it started me wondering. I watched at around the same time each morning hoping to explain how the light was created but it never happened again.

You live on in memory whilst our grandchildren know the stories. They can keep you living in the present. You may have died in physical form but not in spirit. I am happy to say, for those who read our posthumous conversation that in the last ten years of life you were largely able to overcome the difficulties of living with Asperger's and integrate more fully in the world. You became more tolerant of others and more adventurous. I think that after reading about AS symptoms in mid – life, positive change was triggered. Thereafter, there were so many contributors, especially removing alcohol from your life. Improvement in our relationship resulted, and along with the various therapeutic tools mentioned, you managed to integrate your "Cy – Key." Knowledge and understanding finally helped us both make sense of your Asperger's mind.

Walter, so that's how it's done! In the end you created a self that you were happy with, like a beautiful piece of art – a landscape. A good man, you were able to hold onto your centre. Together, we balanced each other, and you gradually found peace in life and in death. Through unconditional love and acceptance, we learned to BE with Asperger's. It was a difficult journey but one I will never regret.

I keep you in my heart and soul forever. Your memory can live on.

And … you must have the last word!

Life would
be a lie
without the
"F" in....

When I died
Death died
too
and I sprang
to life anew.

Printed in the United States
By Bookmasters